MORE

ON THE

PENDLETON

UNDERGROUND

A History of
Pendleton's Underground
and
Pendleton Underground Tours

Pam Severe

Lon Thornburg

ISBN: 0-9743196-0-0

Printed in the United States of America by
Maverick Publications • Bend, Oregon

Introduction

By Pam Severe, Executive Director

It was about 1963 when my parents came home after going underground. Little did I know how that day would influence the rest of my life.

My Dad was a bread distributor who delivered to most of the bars and cafes in Pendleton. Because of that, my parents were able to go underground with Mr. Eng, the owner of a Chinese restaurant, called the Oregon Café. It was located on the east side of Main St. in the middle of the third block, next to the beauty college. My mother Geraldine (Jerry) Severe and my dad, also Jerry Severe, asked if they could go into the basement of the Oregon Cafe and look for old bottles and relics. My mother was an ambitious collector at the time and she had heard rumors that there were a lot of old card rooms and tunnels under the businesses on Main Street. Well, the rumors were true! After entering a trap door in the floor of the cafe and going down some rickety wooden stairs, Mom and Dad found themselves in an old basement, with a bar and card tables. Mom described it as if everyone had just gotten up and left, leaving everything behind. Some chairs were tipped over and cards were all over the floor. On the bar Mother found a treasure—an old beer stein with rubber around the bottom and wax in the center, which came in handy when they would slide the drinks down the bar. Of course she quickly confiscated it. (Today it is displayed in the Shamrock card room). My parents were in awe as they traveled into other areas finding more treasures along the way.

Mr. Eng led them into tunnels built from basalt rock. There, laying in the dirt, was something smooth and white. Mom quickly uncovered a beautiful rectangular-shaped porcelain object with cobalt-blue dragons on the front and Chinese writing on the bottom.

Introduction

It was a box, with an opening on the top. They assumed it was an incense burner, but later found out from a Chinese person in Hermiston, that it was a porcelain pillow. (Now also displayed in the Underground).

The journey became more intriguing as they entered the broad tunnels under the sidewalk. Large sections of purple prism glass, about 3 feet by 4 feet, allowed light into the otherwise pitch-black tunnels. They were amazed at the brilliant light filtering through the glass. There were windows in the walls that allowed the light to also brighten up the adjoining rooms. The squares of glass were spaced about 6 feet apart. Mom and Dad weren't sure where they were heading—one tunnel led to another—until they realized they had gone all the way into the next block on SE 1st. They were still gathering relics along the way, as much as their arms could carry. They didn't ask a lot of questions—they were too busy taking in their surroundings—and before they knew it they were going up another set of old stairs that brought them out into the alley behind the "Oak Hotel", one of Pendleton's bordellos. (This was the same alley that joined the old fire station which was city hall at that time). To get back to where they had started, they had to walk all the way around the block.

That was the story my parents told me when I was about 11 years old. That adventurous story, along with growing up with the relics in our home, made me eager to go underground and see for myself. The next year I turned 12 and walked to the Junior High School located across town on the South hill. We lived on the North hill so I had to walk back and forth to school every day, passing over the glass in the sidewalks and wondering what the other spaces and tunnels were like underground.

We weren't allowed to walk on the west side of Main Street on the block where the Rivoli Theater was because of the bars and shady characters in the area. We did go to movies at the Rivoli, but we weren't allowed to go beyond the theater property. After the movies the kids would line up in front of the theater and their parents would quickly drive by, snatch them up in the cars and take them safely home. Everyone understood the routine and very few kids ever wandered into forbidden territory. After all, the theater was located right in the middle of skid row and the old red light district. I never did get to go underground. Rumors continued of other kids my age sneaking into the tunnels, finding Chinese arti-

Introduction

facts and even hidden passageways that led to Chinese meeting rooms with large statues and other Chinese relics.

I went off to college not giving the underground much more thought. Then, after getting married and having my first child, I returned to Pendleton to start a business. One day in 1989 my mother called me to say that a group of businessmen where trying to get underground tours started in Pendleton's Old Town district and they were having a dinner and fundraiser to get the project started. At last! My opportunity to see the underground! I went to the fundraiser and listened while David Mitzemberg and Phil Garton gave a presentation. At the fundraiser I learned about the Chinese jails, opium dens, and a Cozy room bordello that I had no idea even existed. The work parties had started and the first phase of the tours was ready to open. At the next meeting they took us underground and showed the areas that would be on the tour. It was so interesting! We moved from one space to the next and finally, after going through four rooms, I found myself in the rock tunnels standing under the purple prism glass that I had heard so much about over 25 years ago. The light wasn't as bright as my parent's described, but that was because there was only one section of prism glass remaining in the sidewalk.

The fascination I had for the underground became my vocation in 1990. I took on the responsibility of executive director. My first year was consumed with acquiring props and historic pieces for exhibits and opening phase 2 of the tour in the cozy rooms, Chinese jails and opium den.

I have never tired of hearing new stories from old timers and visitors who hold little pieces of the underground's past in their memories. We have had pin boys from duck pin bowling alleys, old time brothel customers, tunnel explorers, friends and relatives of prominent past families who were building owners, relatives of Hop Sing—Chinese laundryman, etc. The stories and sites underground have come to life through these people who share with us. Thanks to many of them, we have the information to pass on to you in this book.

When deciding a title for the book, I think of how, over the past 12 years, people have come in after visiting on a tour and asked, "Do you have more on the underground?"

So... here it is. For all of you who have patiently waited for a book, here is "More on the Pendleton Underground."

Preface & Acknowledgements

Pendleton Underground Tours (PUT) has had visitors from all over the world. Magazine articles, television interviews and documentaries, have tried to uncover the mystery that surrounds the underground's past. Next to this mystery of the tunnels, one of the most-asked questions is "How did this get started?" Because visitors see the underground and their curiosity is sparked to know more, there have been many requests for a book on the history of the underground and the development of the tours. There has been a need to document the history of how the tours were started and an opportunity to give credit to many of the people who played a part in its beginnings. This book is intended to be one of several on the underground.

Pendleton Underground Tours would like to acknowledge Sonja K. Hart for researching, transcribing and compiling information for PUT to use in this publication.

The Pendleton Underground Tours would like to thank the Jeld-Wen Foundation and Pendleton Foundation Trust for the funding to make this publication possible.

PART ONE

The Town: The Way Things Were
1860's - 1953

Pendleton is rich in history. Although time has taken the past from our view, a living record lives on in the few tunnels that can be enjoyed through the ongoing efforts of Pendleton Underground Tours. While exploring these tunnels, one is transported back to a different time. The sights and sounds and smells of the past fill the senses. It is almost as if ghosts of another era are silently following behind and all around you.

Standing in the tunnels, one can almost hear the clip clop of horses' hooves on the streets above. The laughter and the clinking of glasses still linger in the prohibition card room. The soft laughter of girls and the parlor piano, seem to play in the Cozy Rooms. The tours come to life in a new way once the underground's past is brought to light.

Getting a picture in one's mind of the way it was back then helps to accomplish this.

From well water to fire water

In 1862, Abram Miller became the first settler in the area. He forfeited his opportunity to become a founding father, when he traded 160 acres of land next to the Umatilla River. Moses Goodwin became the beneficiary, trading with Mr. Miller for a span of mules.

Abram Miller, 1860; first settler in area.

Goodwin Station, 1869 on Main Street. Lot Livermore on rooftop, later became first mayor of Pendleton.

Being an entrepreneur, Mr. Goodwin built Goodwin Station along with a toll bridge. From these simple beginnings sprouted up what eventually became "Pendleton."

The simple days of Old Pendleton can be imagined when reading memoirs of Nancy De Spain on village days in Pendleton. Coming out west in 1864, she married and settled 4 miles from Goodwin station at Birch creek in 1866. After 6 years, the family moved into town where Mrs. De Spain begins sharing her fondest memory of the town:

> Well, those were happy days. We housekeepers were certainly self-dependent. There were no bakeries, no laundries, few prepared meats, or vegetables. There were no dairies so we had to keep our own cows, take care of the milk and make the butter. We did not have hot and cold water within arm's reach; no electric lights. About all the help we could get was from the reservation—sometimes a squaw to wash, or an Indian man to work in the garden. We had no time for club or afternoon partie—and little time to read, although many of us loved books and longed for their companionship. But we did enjoy the few diversions we had and we'll never forget them. Do some of you remember the "Old Courthouse Well?" (It was in the northwest corner of the courthouse block) where the People's Warehouse (now Montgomery Ward) stands today.

For those who want a point of reference, the well was located on the corner of Main and Court Street.

> It was to us very attractive, surrounded with a grassy plot—but best of all was the fine, cool water from the depths of the well—different from any in town, we could never account for the difference, unless in digging the well, a spring had been tapped. It was the social center on warm summer evenings. I am sure all the older friends remember it. Men, women and children took the pleasant stroll from their homes to the "Courthouse Well." In addition to the pleasure of the well, we had a good chat with each other—the children romping about in sight of their parents; then home again refreshed! There were no soda fountains, no ice cream parlors, no

3

Old Courthouse. Note well structure on lawn area at corner of Court and Main Street.

"movies." Was it not the simple life? How much the sorrows of our own Pendleton do you think might have never been if the God-given cool, sweet water from the "Old Courthouse Well" had been the only drink procurable from that day to this, outside, of course, of our harmless, innocent home drinks! Well, those were "good old times" and true enough, "there are no friends like the old friends"[1]

The water of the Courthouse Well was pushed aside for new libations as another era hit the little town. The coming of gold in the Blue Mountains brought supply wagon traffic from Umatilla Landing headed for the mining camps. Sheep, cattle and farming began to expand also drawing more people to the area.

By 1899, a town that could be billed as an entertainment capitol, stood to greet Reverend J.M. Cornelison. The young reverend arrived as a new missionary eager to work with the Indians on the reservation. He wrote of the scene that awaited him as he stepped off the train in Pendleton:

I arrived in Pendleton May 5th, 1899. ...Since Pendleton at that time had a population of about 2500, I thought some memories, impressions and happenings to a young tenderfoot who had not cast his first vote, might be of interest and bring a smile to the citizens of such an up and going city of today. As I walked from the sleeper in the early morning hours of that May day up Main Street on the "board walk" (they were all board walks then), I was greeted by the Monterstelli monument works on stilts, that stood over the big hole in the ground about where the Bowman Hotel is now...But the next sight and sign of equal propinquity and juxtaposition to meet and greet me might have been more cheerful to many. There, swung from an arm, extending out over the sidewalk just above my head, was a sign, which read—"The First Chance"—and on the other side it read— "The Last Chance"—if you get what I mean... A large part of the time, the pioneer county court was taken up in granting licenses to sell "liquor" in quantities less than a gallon. They had done a good job of issuing such licenses before I arrived. Out of sheer curiosity I counted such institutions, the results of the court's arduous labors, and they totaled twenty-eight.Or were there thirty-two?"[2]

Pendleton billed itself as "the queen of a golden empire-an empire of golden wheat."[3]

A large farming and livestock region surrounded the town. Cattlemen came from every direction to buy wagonloads of supplies and haul them back to their ranches and camps. Sheep men, "whose herds make white a thousand hills", made Pendleton their trading post. During harvest time, the roads and trails were in a constant state of travel. Thousands of wagons were loaded down with wheat harvested from 200,000 acres. It was described as a procession ever approaching Pendleton. The town was a natural shipping point to send the region's bounty to other cities in the Northwest.[4]

Here are a few figures taken from a Pendleton annual yearbook for 1899-1900:

Four million, five hundred thousand bushels of wheat were one year's crop—one per cent of the national crop at the time.

Two million, five hundred pounds of wool sheared off the sheep's backs was the total wool crop of the area for a single

Woolen mills at shearing time, ca. 1910.

year. This was brought to Pendleton where the local woolen mills increased production of cloth, robes and blankets.

Pendleton was to be "envied" for the railway facility it possessed. It was designed to manage the burst of growth and export of goods from the region. It had a main line East to West, running to Portland, and a line branching North to Walla Walla, Washington.

Growth came quickly to the region. Progress seemed limitless to this turn-of-the-century town. "250 buildings, all solid and substantial, and some exceedingly costly and palatial in design, have been erected in this city in the past eight months."[5]

Entertainment was also a boasting point. "Theatrical and amusement companies make Pendleton a stopping point on their way to or from the East and never fail to play to large houses, a credible opera house affording opportunities for excellent scenic effects."

The city had several classy establishments for its time. Gus La Fontaine, a local restaurateur, was the proprietor of "La Fontaine's French Restaurant." It was equipped with 15 waiters

Frazers Opera House.

to cater to one's every need. Long rows of tables stood with white linens, crystal and silver. The "Owl Tea House" sat on Court Street. It was devoted to the sale of finely blended teas, rare coffees, aromatic spices, flavoring extracts and powders for baking. The store also displayed a wide variety of fine china, silver, crystal and fine crockery. Customers earned a ticket valued at three cents redeemable towards chinaware for every 25 cent purchase.

"Fine Wines, Liquors and Cigars" on Main Street, was known as a "popular resort." The owner, Joseph Hoch, came from St. Louis, spending several years in Astoria, Oregon in the saloon trade. The establishment started in 1885. This was only one of many drinking establishments, saloons and "social resorts."

When one thinks of the vast amounts of wheat harvested and transported and the hundreds of thousands of pounds of wool sheared, the labor force has to be considered in order to make this possible. The labor force would have consisted of thousands of men. One wheat harvest team with draft horse-drawn harvest equipment and the harvesting crew, would have employed up to

Wheat Harvest Crew.

100 men. Shepherds and sheep shearing on the scale that is recorded for the time, would have involved hundreds of men. Add in all the wagon drivers and muscle power to load and unload freight to mining camps and cow camps, and a person begins to see the amount of masculine thirst and appetite there was to be satisfied in the saloons and brothels of Pendleton.

In its heyday, before restrictions, Pendleton became the town of choice for a good time in Umatilla County. 32 card rooms and bars and 18 brothels, kept the men happy.

"Saloons and dance halls were in abundance, thronged all night with open gambling for high stakes. The floors, after a long siege of poker, would be covered with decks of cards discarded by unfortunate players. Yet, with all this, Pendleton was never a wild or disorderly town. These things occurred as a matter of course and as the custom of the country and created but little excitement or comment."[6]

Saloons had names like "The Olympia" and "The Elk Horn".

"The Louvre" was started by one of the town's brewers, John Schmidt. It was one of the town's most popular drinking establishments. Even the name lent refinement to its atmosphere and customers. The owner had a sample room where domestic and imported wines and liquors could be tasted.

"The State" and "Banquet" Saloons were known for the hospitality of the proprietor, Ed C. Allen. These saloons were known as "people places", where you went for good company.

"August Stangiers'" boasted a "mixologist" of ability and skill. The two were popularized locally as being jovial and well liked. "The wine placed upon his bar sparkles like a ruby red and has the aroma of an Italian vineyard; the beer he serves reflects in its amber depths the golden Wisconsin sunset; the well-aged whisky brings up visions of the glad Kentucky hills and still has clinging to it her sweetest mountain air."[7]

"J.B.Damain, liquor Dealer," was an establishment with a Belgian proprietor. It was touted as a quiet, social establishment. The saloon was on a "prominent corner in one of the neatest little brick buildings in the city."

9

Roesch Brewery.

Because there was no refrigeration at that time, beer could not be shipped. Each town had to have its own brewery. Pendleton had seven breweries and one distillery. One of the liquor stores had its own brewery in the basement and there were two others in basements.[8]

The best known brewery of the time was owned by William Roesch. The City Brewery and City Brewery Saloon were taken over by Mr. Roesch in 1881, and he was reputed to stick with the industry through ups and downs and thick and thin. He kept his brewery running, turning out 20 barrels or 600 gallons of beer daily, ALL of which were consumed at home in Pendleton. The town appreciated the local employment, use of local grains and crops, and the money spent on the actual beer kept the money here in the community. It was an early example of the economic "trickle down" effect.

The standard set-up was to house card rooms under a saloon in the basement. Drinking establishments served their customers on the main floor and the upstairs was commonly reserved for the bordello areas.

There were at least 18 brothels operating in Pendleton from the late 1890's through 1953, when all were shut down.

Prohibition started in Pendleton in 1908. At that time only 12 saloons were allowed to continue operating. Stories of underground drinking rooms and escape tunnels began to appear from this date onward throughout the United States enforced prohibition period of 1916-1933. These stories told of barrels of bootleg alcohol being rolled down tunnels to be sold, card rooms with secret back rooms, escape routes, whisky and beer runners, bootleggers, etc.

County sheriffs enforced local law until 1912, when Til Taylor became the first local sheriff and began to enforce the prohibition law more strictly. Still, we know that a certain tolerance persisted and an eye would look the other way in many cases. Raids were publicized and used to appease the local population disapproving of the vices hidden in the community.

The end of prohibition in 1933 gave many reasons to celebrate, but events were leading towards WWII.

The building of an airbase in Pendleton in late 1939–early 1940, brought a new customer to Pendleton. The airman in uniform now joined the dusty, thirsty cowboy and sheepherder.

In 1942, Pendleton's airbase became a key place where the war department recruited seasoned pilots for The Dolittle's Raiders. This elite corp. was trained to retaliate against Japan by flying a risky bombing raid after the attack on Pearl Harbor. The impact this had on the town was tremendous.

One impact was the change that came in the names of the downtown streets. Before 1939, in the neighborhood of what is now the home of P.U.T., Emigrant Street was named Webb. Dorion was Alta and SW 1st was Garden Street. The Underground tours are conducted under the block that was Garden and Webb, and Webb and Main (old names).

The brothels in this area were kept busy, as were the drinking establishments. The duck pin bowling alley and billiards under

Still Room. First probibition in Pendleton was in 1908 which brought about bootleggers making moonshine in still rooms.

Prohibition, ca. 1918-20. Note Til Taylor, Pendleton's first sheriff, standing behind barrel. Famous champion black cowboy, George Fletcher, fourth person to the right, watches in background.

Barrel of whisky from previous photo being poured in the gutter. Early caption for photo said: "Mourners joined officials at this typical prohibition era scene. A barrel of moonshine was about to be sent gurgling down the gutter. Sheriff Til Taylor officiated and a deputy, seen carrying a brace and bit, drilled a hole that let the liquor flow out." Author unknown.

Til Taylor, Pendleton's first sheriff.

The New York Store kept active with airmen looking for amusement and recreation off the base.

Vera Simonton, Pendleton resident, recalled for Pendleton Underground Tours her memories of the brothels and ladies that were employed upstairs in the Hendricks Building. She was a clerk in the late 1940's and early '50's at The New York Store on the corner of Main and Emigrant, which was above the prohibition card room and duck pin bowling alley on the underground tour. She recalled the working girls doing business with railroad workers who were boarding upstairs above the store in the rooms that are now The Working Girls Hotel. The girls had apartments across the hall above the Empire Meat market.

The "red light" district of Pendleton evolved through the years and saw much change. The streets changed from an early accepted saloon and card room district to hidden speak-easies

Pendleton Air Field, ca. 1942.

and prohibition card rooms behind the doors and in basements of reputable businesses. Brothels and cozy rooms were in business from Pendleton's beginning in the 1800's throughout the 1930's and '40's. Even this was to change in 1953 when all the working girls were escorted out of town one night.

When one considers the wildness and recklessness of Pendleton's bawdy past, it is hard to imagine that she could ever be tamed. When visitors explore the tunnels, the question always arises, "When did all this end?" or "Why did all this end?" The west was a hard place to tame, but eventually civilization came to every corner. Pendleton's history shows many hardworking people striving to bring Pendleton into the 20th century with a new level of civility and class. Immoral behavior was to be crowded out by a desire for propriety—even by the men who once visited the old establishments.

An example of some citizens opinions of seedy business dealings can be taken from an 1895 editorial in *The East Oregonian* newspaper. The following incident transpired after its printing.

The editor, Mr. Jackson, was critical of a Mr. Hendricks' (builder of the Hendricks Building) opposition to voting for an annual school tax. Mr. Hendricks stated his opposition of a public school tax by saying that he would spend up to twenty dollars of his own money to campaign for its defeat. E.O. Editor, Mr. Jackson wrote this of Hendricks in his column:

> Mr. Hendricks is abundantly able to spend twenty dollars in this way. He secured many twenty dollar gold pieces from the renting of bawdy houses. Since his income is largely derived from this source, it is natural for him to expend some of it against the maintenance of public schools, which have the effect of decreasing the demand for such houses.[9]

This ended up in a physical altercation between the editor and Hendricks on the street. Hendricks called Jackson a liar. Jackson slapped Hendricks. Hendricks hit Jackson with his cane. Hendricks was arrested for using profane and offensive language on the street and fined $20.

More on the Pendleton Underground

With the brothels closing in 1953, underground activity also seemed to taper down. Even though there was a working brothel in Pendleton until 1965 and various back rooms for cards and gaming, the stronghold of the underground had passed on.

The city added to and updated blocks and their utilities. Refrigeration eliminated the need for ice and cool storage areas. Many tunnels were closed in basements and filled with water, gas and sewer lines. Electrical conduit and cables took the place of shuffling Chinese workers and bootleggers.

We look at the underground as something mysterious, exciting and unique. The bootleggers, card dealers, Chinese and the men who paid for their trade and services, looked at the underground as a commonplace necessity. Through the years, the stories and activities of the underground became an embarrassing part of Pendleton's past. The bordellos and saloons of the red light district became skid row. The glamour was gone and so was any interest in preserving the past. The underground's history might have been lost forever if it hadn't been for the efforts of a few men who started Pendleton Underground Tours.

PART TWO

The Tours: The Way Things Started
1987 - Present

A group of rowdy young adventurers in the 1960's and '70's heard stories of Pendleton's past. Knowing there were tunnels under the town, they would spend late Saturday nights with friends exploring downtown basements to find secret doors and mysterious tunnels. Out of this group of friends, eventually started Pendleton Underground Tours.

From Pub Crawls to Board Members

The initial group that founded the tours, had the task of putting together the puzzle of where the tunnels went and what went on there. Uncovering the stories of what had been hidden for so long was not easy.

Dave Mitzemberg, Phil Garton, and Greg Brooks were the first to break ground in this area. These men had a curiosity about the tunnels and wanted to get to the bottom of what went on there. It was at a pub crawl in the late 1980's, where some of the men mentioned above found themselves going down into the bar basements and tunnels with old timers, who began to swap stories. It was at this time the founders of PUT realized there was much more to the underground than they ever imagined. It

Dave Mitzemberg, early founder, performing as sheepherder in Shamrock Card Room during PUT Comes To Life. AKA Rufus Crabtree.

Kirt Skinner, Buford Kinnison & Phil Garton

was so much fun hearing the tales and being in the actual spaces where they occurred that they wanted to share the experience with others. Out of this came the idea to clean up the tunnels through cooperation with the property owners and start a tour to take people through those tunnels. The idea seemed to be one that could really become a popular local attraction...IF it could be done at all.

Not only did these men have to find the information and interview countless residents—now in their 80's and 90's, but they would also have to coordinate volunteer manpower to clean out tons of broken brick, rock, mortar, coal, and years of junk that had been thrown into these basements. At this time, Bert Arndt owned The Empire Building and The Hendricks Building. (See Part Four for photos.) These two buildings had tunnels that seemed to be the most intact, and possibly suited for future tour potential. It was found that these tunnels contained Chinese rock-

19

work, a prohibition card room and an escape tunnel. Mr. Arndt listed these buildings in the early 1980's, as part of a National Historic Registry project for Pendleton's Main Street. With his consent, the work could commence. Kirt Skinner was an invaluable resource in heading up the construction and restoration of the tunnels. Even though things were coming together, there were still obstacles to deal with above ground.

There were citizens that wanted the "seedy" past of Pendleton to remain buried to protect the town's image. These citizens had lived here their whole lives and insisted that none of the tunnels, brothels or card rooms ever existed. They didn't want to accept the shameful fact that this could be part of their community's history. There were property owners that had a family name and a reputation to uphold. Some of their ancestors had made profits from the shady activities and businesses that took place where the underground tours operate today. These investment property owner-ancestors had gained income from saloons, card rooms and brothels. They had kept their business practices and ill-reputed gains more or less hidden from public scrutiny.

The shame of Pendleton's past didn't help the early PUT founders bring it to light. To overcome this obstacle, the underground tour concept had to be presented in a manner that was pleasing to the public. It had to be brought out in a tasteful manner.

The PUT founders held community dinners to present the project to interested leaders in the community. They took these people below to see the work in progress and shared some stories. When they had seen the underground and heard the concept of the tours, and how it would be presented, a blessing was bestowed. The effects of this early public relations effort brought a lot of local support. City employees assisted in rerouting a sewer main that ran down the middle of the basements. City crews had to dig up part of the street and lay pipe several feet below ground level. Other assistance began to come in from local businesses in the way of labor and materials. Volunteer crews patched walls and built new walls and hallways. A doorway was cut in one basement wall to connect to other areas. Some doorways were broken through and other doorway sections bricked in. Walls were broken through, supports secured and concrete poured. Pipes and wiring at shoulder height had to be raised, re-plumbed and re-wired. Donated funding paid contractors to do what volunteer labor couldn't. Fire and safety concerns had to be given top priority. City employees provided assistance in getting these issues solved and the tours ready for opening. It took 133 days for volunteer crews, business owners and the Boy Scouts to clean out and prepare the tour space areas in order for the work to be completed.

There was a healing process underway in this entire effort. Town support and volunteer contributions allowed Pendleton to make it a community tour—not just the underground's tour. The ownership and cooperation of all parties let the city have a part in "revealing" its past.

One of the hardest struggles facing PUT was the opening of the Cozy Rooms, Stella Darby's brothel, which was closed in 1953. In 1990, one year after the opening of a phase 1 tour in the underground portion, a phase 2 was to be added. This phase would add the Cozy Rooms upstairs and an opium den and Chinese jails in the basements of the Medernach Building. The Lorenzen's owned this building and had owned it throughout occupancy by Stella Darby. When it was closed in 1953, the owners took out the red light that hung inside, above the front entrance on Main Street. Further remodeling was done to hide the original double doors and painted windows. The front entry was enclosed in brick and mortar. The back fire escape stairs were taken down to seal up any exterior access to the building. The only entrance was a side door inside the front entry that was accessed through a room next door. The upstairs was virtually sealed off from 1953 until 1990 when Celia Lorenzen finally gave consent for its use. Up until this time, it had been accessed for storage only. This is how many of the properties ended up in the downtown Pendleton area. Getting the history and use of these places, as well as being able to share it with the public, involved convincing property owners that information would be shared tastefully and that it would be a way of opening up the past to visitors and create more tourism for the community.

The involvement, approval and the blessing of the towns-people, as well as the undergrounds' exposure of Pendleton's history, has helped in healing some of the shame associated with the past.

With the local people's objections overcome and the prep work completed underground, the tours were really beginning to become a reality.

After the initial cleaning and preparing of the tunnels and rooms, the task of acquiring antiques and decorating came next. Donated furnishings and collectibles were put in place. Salvaged articles from the underground clean up work were placed on display. The first tours did not see the amount of artifacts available to visitors today. Over the past decade there has been a constant and continual acquiring by executive director, Pam Severe. Funding for these acquisitions has come through grants and tour proceeds.

In September of 1989, the doors opened for the week of the annual Pendleton Round-Up. The response was tremendous and more than anyone could have imagined. That first year finished with over 12,000 people having explored Pendleton's underground tour.

The opening of the Cozy Rooms, Chinese jails and opium den in 1990, completed the tour PUT wanted visitors to experience in the effort to share a part of Pendleton's past.

Since its origin in 1987, Pendleton Underground Tours has been a non-profit corporation dedicated to the preservation of Pendleton's underground history. A by-product of this has become the contribution to tourism and the economic picture in the community.

The tours have drawn over 150,000 visitors since it opened. PUT has drawn cruise ships on the Columbia River to the underground and Pendleton. The executive director of PUT, Pamela Severe, has worked together with the Chamber of Commerce to provide tours in town that utilize the Round-Up grounds, convention center, Pendleton Woolen Mills, and local musicians and western entertainers, to create a draw for tourism beyond the week of the famous Pendleton Round-Up.

In 1994, a charitable donation was given as seed money to start the vision of The Confederated Tribes of the Umatilla Indian Reservation for Tamastslikt, the Native American interpretive center outside of Pendleton. PUT helped in initial support and organization in an effort to raise funds and awareness of the need for a Native American cultural center. PUT assisted in the support and coordination of the sesquicentennial celebration of The Oregon Trail when the wagon trains came through Pendleton in 1993.

The purchase, restoration and development by PUT of the three historic buildings standing above the main portion of the tours, also in 1993, demonstrated a large commitment to the city and its future.

Pendleton Underground Tour's "Comes To Life," was started as an annual fundraising event. Each year for one day, local participants take on period costumes and fill the underground and Cozy rooms with life and laughter to delighted guests. Usually sold out in advance, the day raises funds, which help in the operation costs, preservation of the historical properties and development of future PUT projects. This annual event also draws many visitors to the community for the weekend of the event.

Oregon Public Broadcasting has brought the underground to statewide television. The History Channel brought PUT national attention in documenting the underground as part of a 2 hour program, "Secret Passages" in 2000. Funding has been granted by many, including, Pendleton Foundation Trust, Union Pacific Foundation, Meyer Memorial trust, and The Jeld-Wen Foundation. This funding has been used to enhance the tours and develop new areas.

There is so much yet to be discovered and the future promises to bring much more for visitors to explore on Pendleton Underground Tours.

PART THREE

Tunnel Tales: Tall Tales & True Tales

An urban legend-type history had sprung up in the community over the years. The common story would start: "So and so" knew someone who had been in a tunnel and found..." which led to gigantic distortions that were far from the truth, yet fun to tell. A few of the common misconceptions and underground tall tales were:

"If all of Pendleton's underground tunnels were laid out in one long line, they would stretch over 150 miles in length."

"The underground tunnels were built exclusively for the Chinese to move secretly from one space to another."

"The tunnels ran under the Eastern Oregon Psychiatric Center (mental hospital), delivering supplies on small railroad tracks in the hospital basement."

"The Original Happy Canyon Grounds had wagon wheel spoke-like tunnels (moving out like catacombs under the Roman Coliseum) that went to Main Street; north to Umatilla Landing; under the river and up the hill to a basement in a house on NW Carden; south to the cliffs, and another easterly towards the Catholic Church."

25

"Tunnels existed coming out in basements of houses in the East part of town."

"A rail car on a track in town, fell through the street into a tunnel below."

"Airplanes would land at the airstrip at night and smugglers would roll bootleg barrels and other contraband down long tunnels that ran from the airport to the red light district downtown."

These stories are fun to hear and have been documented in the local *East Oregonian Newspaper* and even compiled in a book. We may reprint some of the stories here, but one must remember that we cannot take these as literal truth. Most of the tunnels have been sealed or destroyed and the opportunity to provide proof went with them. The stories are an important part of oral tradition and for that reason have a place in our history. When you take out the distortions and far-flung tales, one common denominator stands true, there WERE tunnels and lots of interesting things happened there.

The following story is paraphrased from "The Pendleton Story," now out of print, which is dedicated to preserving the legends and stories told by old timers of Pendleton's underground. These stories are shared in the above-mentioned spirit, knowing you will take it with a grain of salt...and a smile.

Haunted Tunnels

Back in the late 1890's there were a pair no-good thugs named Snake and Preachin' Sam.

These two heard stories about the tunnels in Pendleton while drinking in the saloons. One story in particular was about a tunnel that went from the caretakers shed in Pioneer Cemetery, under the street, to a trap door in the basement of a house across the street. The two decided that this would be a great hideout while they held up stores and banks. They bought off the caretakers that lived in the house, talking them into letting the two stay there.

After the two had basically "house-jacked" the place, they found 6 guns to ride with them and began their heists. They would ride out of town, leave a trail to follow and then double back and hide the stash in the tunnel and lay low in the basement. This went on while they robbed gold shipments leaving Pendleton every Friday after the miners made their deposits.

After five robberies, the gang decided on one last big job— a train robbery. As they plotted and planned, the people upstairs overheard the conversation. They felt hostage in their own home and began to make their own plans.

The night of the big train robbery, the gang came back to the cemetery with over $100,000 in gold they had stolen. They unloaded the gold into the tunnel and went down under only to find that the people who lived in the house had been waiting for them in the tunnel with guns, prepared to take the loot. A shootout occurred underground. The two groups argued, shouting loudly, "It's MY gold!", "No! It's MY gold!" They shot at each other late into the night until every one of them was dead.

The legend goes on to say that a week later, the sheriff found the tunnel under the house and the gold, but no bodies to explain who put it there. New caretakers that moved into the house reported that they had heard shots ringing out in the basement and ghostly voices shouting "It's my gold!" When the ghostly gun battle thundered up the stairs, the new residents reported that the ghosts chased each other, their guns blazing, right through the walls of the house and disappeared into thin air. Needless to say the new residents packed up and left.

The house is no longer standing today, but people still say if you are out in the cemetery on a quiet night, you can still hear gunshots and arguing over the gold coming from tunnels somewhere down below.[10]

The following stories are examples of tales based on facts that cannot be proven because of tunnels that have been sealed and destroyed. More than one person has verified the stories you are about to read. They were there, were involved, or spoke with an actual participant. One of the actual explorers in one of the stories came in to the Underground Tours office and gave us his account. Several of these were also printed in *The Pendleton Story*, now out of print. We tell these stories based on facts provided to us by locals, stories from the actual "Perpetrators" and *The Pendleton Story*.

Chinese Tunnels and Buddhas

Chinese artifacts in tunnels have helped to substantiate that the Chinese lived and worked for a time in Pendleton's underground. Two sets of young men apparently made identical discoveries unbeknownst to each other in the 1970's. If we could have gone down and found these places while still intact, it would have given us more information on the Chinese in Pendleton.

One of these young men, (we'll call Jon), and a friend, were in Crabby's back when it was Rathskellers, having a few drinks. The store above, now Blue Mountain Sports, had been The Vintage Shoppe and was being remodeled—so things were torn up.

Jon said he knew how to get into the basement of The Vintage Shoppe through a hole in the wall behind the furnace in the basement of Crabby's. He said there was another hole in The Vintage Shoppe basement that led to tunnels that went under the streets of town. The two sneaked into the furnace room and found the hole. They crawled through into the adjoining basement where they looked for a tunnel entrance. They found a working flashlight left in the basement. With this help they were able to find the hole that was the tunnel entrance.

> We entered a hole in the East side of the basement wall and went into a tunnel. It looked more like a meeting room than a tunnel. There were books, grass mats, plates and saucers. A Buddha, and writing on the wall. The tunnel went under Main Street and intersected with another tunnel that ran North and South under the sidewalk on the opposite side of the block. We decided not to venture any further and came back. We stopped and picked up a few artifacts as we left."[11]

Now, the owner of Blue Mountain Sports had reported that this story was NOT a rumor because the individual, (Jon), had come in and told him the story and asked if he could go down and see if the hole was still there and pick up some more artifacts. The hole had been blocked up for years and when the two went to look behind the furnace... sure enough, a patched up hole was there.

Another account of similar findings surfaced a few years later. A story had made the rounds telling of mazes, golden Buddhas, a temple room, Chinese dishes, etc. In 1994, a man in his forties came into the Underground Tours and asked the tour director if she had ever heard the story about the Buddha and Chinese tunnels. Pam Severe, the executive director, told him yes, but that we didn't tell it on the tours because it could not be verified. The man said, "I was one of the guys that crawled in there and I saw it...it's a fact."

Here's what he told the director:

He and a friend had sneaked into the basement of the Temple Hotel. They had heard stories of tunnels and had heard they could be accessed through the Temple Hotel basement. The hotel basement had been shut down and was full of junk they had to crawl through and over. They found a doorway through the North side of the basement wall. On the other side was a tunnel with glass blocks in the ceiling. They were under the Main Street sidewalk. Even though it was night, the street lights magnified through the glass so they could easily see their way. They found quite a few tunnels that went under the street to the west and some that led east under the block. They followed the tunnel north down Main Street 3 blocks, all the way to the tunnel that led under Blue Mountain Sports.

The tunnel floor began to get wet and the farther north (towards the river) they went, the more water they began to find, so they turned back. When they got to the tunnel that crossed under Main Street to Blue Mountain Sports, they decided to take a look. In this tunnel they found writing on the walls that they couldn't read. They came across grass mats, books, incense, a

Temple Hotel above ground, along SE First Street. Note prism glass panels in sidewalk to light underground tunnels.

Temple Hotel underground, same area. Not seen on tours.

Local Chinese man Mr. Loo, (on right). Ca. 1900.
Well known for his laundry business.

big statue that looked like a Buddha, bottles, etc. They found a hole that took the tunnel on into another room, but were afraid they would get lost if they kept going in different tunnels, so they went back to the Temple Hotel basement and crawled out onto the street level, back into the fresh air.

In *The Pendleton Story*, the author writes an account of a woman who was having lunch at the Red Lion in the late 1980's. A waiter overheard her talking about the underground area and stopped to visit with her. He told her that he and a friend had been under the Temple Hotel a while back and the things he described down there were found to be the same things as mentioned above.[12]

Whether this was "the friend" of the man that came into the PUT office, or another incident altogether, we'll never know. The names of these people have been protected for the obvious reason that there was trespassing involved.

The historian/tour guides on Pendleton Underground Tours are given material that stays within the realm of researched fact. Over the years, the tour guide script has been edited to exclude things that might sound good but have no credibility.

It has been difficult to research and find exact dates for many of the things that happened underground. City records do not show dates of construction on the tunnels. The shady activities that took place underground were certainly not going to be recorded in any books. The knowledge we have has had to come through interviews that have been transcribed for our archives. These interviews, when possible, have been cross-checked and verified with other people's interviews and memoirs. We are fortunate to have *Reminiscences of Oregon Pioneers* published by The Pioneer Ladies Club of Pendleton in 1937 and *A Century of News and People in the East Oregonian, 1875-1975*, published by *The East Oregonian Newspaper*, Pendleton. We have pulled much from these sources as well as information from letters and correspondence with the surviving relatives of people we know knew of the tunnels and what went on there.

Here are some stories and accounts that verify the where-abouts of certain tunnels and the activities that went on there. They have been documented and confirmed by at least two oral accounts from separate sources.

The Main Street Tunnel System

We have reason to believe that one of the original purposes of the tunnels design and construction was for transporting supplies and strongboxes of gold and cash safely underneath the streets to various basements. These items could then be taken upstairs into stores, banks, businesses, and hotels.

Each of the eight blocks running four to each side along Main Street, were encircled under the sidewalk with a tunnel. Each tunnel had a "walk-way" along its length lit by prism glass blocks. These tunnels ran parallel to the sidewalks above, all the way around the block. In the tunnels, there were doorways entering the basements, coinciding with the businesses above. Each basement had a front doorway and had a set of windows and some had bars for security. The windows allowed the light to flood into the basements just as windows lit the main floors upstairs. Each basement had a back door and front door for going out the tunnel that lined the back block behind Main Street on SW First or SE First. The front walls of the tunnels along each business basement were brick and stonework, looking as nice as their counterparts on the street above. When deliveries were made, hand trucks could be rolled down the "sidewalk" underground, and the deliveries could be made through the doorways into the basements of the businesses. The underground was almost a mirror image of Main Street above, with well-lit passageways, store basement entrances, complete with arched windows.

Before cement sidewalks the boardwalks had iron grills, which allowed fresh air and sunlight down into the tunnels. When the wood was replaced with cement, panels of depression glass were inserted in place of the grills to magnify and create better light. This also prevented wind, rain and water run-off from coming down into the tunnels.

The train depot was a starting point and drop-off point for an underground delivery system. There used to be a different depot at the turn of the century that sat closer to Main Street and the Bowman Hotel. A tunnel ran from the train depot under Frazer to The Bowman Hotel. Goods could also be taken underground at the site of The Empire Building where PUT is today. From there, they could go across under Main Street to the Temple Hotel, or down the West side of Main Street towards the river and cross in other places. We have no real documentation of tunnels extending past the eight Main Street blocks into other areas of town. There are rumors of tunnels going under the river, up the North hill, and from the Catholic Church to the old hospital.

In 2001, Jerry LaGore told PUT about a tunnel that started in the basement of the Catholic Church and his story has been backed up by others in the community.

The Catholic Church had a gas smell in the basement due to a service station tank that was leaking. When the gas smell was tracked down, it came from a large space behind a basement wall. It was found to be a tunnel. The tank had seeped gas into it over time. The service station cleaned up the mess and the church sealed over the tunnel permanently. There were those who said the gas smell and the dangerous looking state of the tunnel kept anyone from exploring where it led. Speculation and stories tell that the tunnel was a safe passage for the sisters to the church from the hospital and academy on what was then part of the Umatilla Indian Reservation.

Mr. LaGore also told about tunnels built for mill race. Portions of the mill races were underground tunnels made of brick and stone that served as underwater aqua ducts from the Umatilla River to the wool mill and flour mill. Jerry had to go into one of the tunnels as a young man and do repair/cleaning work on a section. He described it as well built but claustrophobic. Rumors have it that flooding caused one section of the mill race to get covered over and diverted in a way that it was no longer used for water and became a human-use tunnel, crossing under the Umatilla River from downtown to access the North Hill.

The tunnels were convenient for working girls and men seeking their company. Whether it was a working girl visiting a hotel room, or a customer getting to a brothel unseen, the tunnel routes conveniently allowed secret passages to and from the brothels and hotels. Alleyways and basements allowed easy access to these tunnels day and night. The Bowman Hotel was accessed through a tunnel under the Empire building, now closed off, allowing the girls to pass under the street, avoiding drunk and rowdy men that might harass them. This also kept the hotel from getting a bad reputation.

Chinatown, Opium Dens and More Tunnel Stories

Visitors to the underground always have questions about why the Chinese were here and how many. An East Oregonian publication explains:

> The main line that put Umatilla on the transcontinental map had come through early in the decade. Tracks of the Oregon Railway and Navigation Company reached Pendleton from Umatilla on September 11, 1882.[13]

In the same year of 1882, U.S. Congress responded to anti-Chinese sentiment in the West. Because Chinese immigrants were willing to work for less than whites, resentment arose as white Americans felt their job security threatened. The Chinese Exclusion Law of 1882 was designed to protect the rights and employment of American workers.

It prevented Chinese workers, whether skilled in a trade or unskilled, from working in mining or any employment that would "steal" that work from an American citizen. This only left service jobs such as cleaning, laundry, and cooking. This is why we see these occupations as the "stereotyped" trade of the early Chinese immigrant in the West.

Early in 1891 mobs began driving Chinese laborers out of railroad work camps. At Milton, on January 22 of that year, about a hundred white railroad section workers went to the quarters of the Chinese workers, put ropes around their necks and hauled them out of town. Two were so roughly treated they needed medical help. This was stimulant to other white workers and Chinese were driven from their jobs in Weston, Adams and Athena where railroad building was underway. This threat was felt because the Chinese worked hard and asked little in the way of adequate housing or pay. Chinese laundrymen of whom there were many, were not molested. At that time Pendleton had no Chinese railroad workers although there were many Chinese in town—in 1890 the number was estimated at 90.[14]

At the turn of the century, a "Chinatown" and Chinese activity were thriving. Census figures show that in 1870, 9 Chinese were counted. In 1880 - 21; in 1900 - 82; and in 1910 there were 50. Jobs ranged from cooks to laborers, laundry and lodging houses. We know that the actual population was beyond a census count. Many Chinese were not included in a local census. They didn't want to be counted or noticed. The *East Oregonian* of May 31, 1893 had the following article of interest:

> Deputy Sheriff Durham has so far collected about $49 in poll taxes from Pendleton Chinese, who are charged $1 a head. He encountered very little kicking, as the wily celestial is aware that these are times when stubbornness is not part of wisdom. Last year the Chinese were very independent and only $33 could be collected."

PUT archives and interviews have turned up some interesting stories.

Based on accounts by Morse Temple, longtime resident now deceased, the area where Bank of America now sits, used to be the site of a large building that was part of a small Chinatown. The building next door to the South of the bank is still standing. It evidently used to have a noodle house upstairs, several Chinese laundries and living quarters. The tunnels underneath that area of the block had several opium dens. A fire destroyed the large building on the corner in the 1920's and exposed the tunnels underneath. A person could see the wood bunks and buckets used in the opium dens. (Their location was similar to the way the opium den is seen on the Underground Tour.)

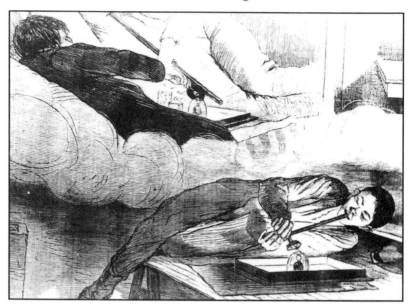

Opium den drawing illustrating reclining positions for smoking opium.

Waible Patton, long time resident, shared his memories of Pendleton's Chinatown.

Chinese laborers were the "earth movers" during the construction of the railroads in the west. When the railroads were finished, a goodly number of the Chinese settled right here in Pendleton. The block from which Payless recently moved (now the site of Bank of America), was completely covered with their old wooden buildings as was the block where the post office now stands. One other block across the street from Payless was included. Quite a few of the Chinese made their living by opening Chinese laundries.[15]

Elmer Pozegar, resident since 1912, told PUT of his memories concerning Pendelton's "Chinatown". He remembered it being from The Odd Fellows Hall, down SW 1st on both sides. Of the opium dens and Chinese gangs, called tongs, he recalled:

The head Chinaman's name was Ung Doj Goey and he was the leader of the Chinese people. He was also high ranking in the Hip Sing Tong. Word had gotten around that a rival tong was sending a "hatchet man" down to kill him, (Ung Doj Goey), so he just packed up and moved. No one saw him again. Two days later they found a man in the entrance of a tunnel cut from his neck to his chest with a hatchet. The people figured that the man sent down from the rival tong couldn't find Ung Doj Goey, so he left a message for him.

From what Elmer could remember, the Chinese seemed to have left a few days after this happened. They all just seemed to desert their living quarters and disappear. The buildings stayed empty for a while, then other people moved into them.

He recalled visiting an opium den and remembered the woodwork being black with smoke. He heard that the Chinese would go down and smoke the opium for an hour and then either meditate or go to sleep. This seemed to be their idea of relaxing.

In 1994, an underground study committee researched local records and interviewed citizens for any history of the Chinese in Pendleton. Andy Bellomo of Pendleton, verified that several Chinese lived in a building on the corner where Bank of America stands today. As a youth he recalled seeing them read Chinese newspapers. There was a Chinese barbershop in the area and one of the barbers was a lady. Mr. Bellomo said the men liked to go to her to get their faces patted by a lady. He said there was a Chinese restaurant upstairs.

Waible Patton reminisced about the Chinese New Year celebrations and the fireworks displays they had. He recalled that the Chinese didn't hesitate to make money by supplying the townspeople all the firecrackers they wanted for the Fourth of July. He says:

> The Chinese brought many of their customs along with them including celebration of their new year. We helped them celebrate it—at least the firecracker part...they reciprocated on our Fourth of July by importing fireworks and selling them to us. So many firecrackers were set off down on Main Street that the refuse from their paper coverings hid the cobblestones and presented a real fire hazard as more and

more were set off amid the rubble. Main Street at that time was a dirt street covered with cobblestones, prone to mud or dust. They (the firecrackers) sometimes set fire to the paper rubble in the street and this is actually what was responsible for the fire that burned out one whole block of Chinatown one Fourth of July.[16]

The Chinese have been credited with building many basalt rock basements, service tunnels, house foundations and retaining walls throughout Pendleton. The only record found concerning the Chinese and any building of tunnels or excavating work is found in an article from the *East Oregonian* dated October 2, 1893. The Chinese were excavating on Webb Street for sewer pipe to lead from their wash-house on Webb, near Garden, to the mill stream. Some complaints were made, but most councilmen thought it was best to let the Chinese run off the wash water than to allow it to stand and become stagnant in a cesspool and germinate diseases. The census of 1900 showed 12 of these Chinese laundry houses in business.

Gambling and opium were underground attractions run by the Chinese. Regular sweeps through town were made by law officials to fine and arrest offenders. According to local municipal court dockets, opium dens were raided from 1904 up through 1923. Fines and arrests varied. Arrests were made for smoking opium and the fine was $25; running an opium joint or house, $40. Municipal records show Mr. Ung Doj Goey, mentioned earlier, was arrested for operating gambling establishments in 1906 and again in 1907. A woman was arrested in July 1907 and fined $25 for smoking opium.

Sweeps of the city's opium dens would result in arrests and fines of $25 to $40 in 1907.

During WWI, in 1916, $100 fines were charged for running opium dens. The last record was a Sung Tie, who was arrested for smoking opium in 1921, but charges were dismissed.

It is important to note that the earliest Chinese residents were never considered trouble-makers and probably handled most of their problems within their own community. Many of the Chinese who settled permanently in Pendleton became associated with the restaurant business and their success is reflected in the fact that some of the families were operating these restaurants up until the mid twentieth century.[17]

The Globe Café on Main Street was a Chinese restaurant up through the early 1960's. This restaurant was next to The Cozy rooms. The Verstoppens owned the café and shared with PUT that under the café in the basement was an office room left over from Chinese owners. It contained old papers with a lot of Chinese writing. There was a sealed door in the room that looked like it went under the sidewalk. The owner forced open the door and found a storage room of sorts filled with Chinese pots, jars and old restaurant supplies. The ceiling in this room contained the prism glass panels seen on the tour today.

On a shelf, the owner found an antique silk Chinese gown wrapped in paper. The gown was on loan on display in The Underground Tours display area for several years. The gown was blue with gold thread and embroidery work. The underground office and room mentioned above are still there today. They are adjacent to the last room on the current underground tour, under the sidewalk. The opium den, Chinese jails and community living area on the underground tour underwent archaeological analysis in 1992. The opium den area had extensive items that told about the room, the use and the people who used it.

J.S. Reed, field archaeologist, dug from August 22 to September 4, 1992. He was able to find layers of soil representing years 1903-1915. The areas he uncovered revealed more women's apparel and jewelry than men's. Earrings, broaches, hatpins, hair combs and rings were found. His deduction was that many women were down in the room, perhaps prostitutes with opium addictions. Coins were found, none deeper than soil dated 1918. The probable betting-line amount of the gamblers at the time seemed to be a dime based on coins found—equivalent to the buying power of $3 today. Shattered disks, chips and tokens, glass shards (some porcelain), wooden matches and a very old thin pipe consistent with opium smoking, were found. Old motion picture ticket stubs at 5 & 10 cent admission prices were in the area suggesting...movies and gambling afterwards? Ash and burnt wood indicated a small wood stove had been used in the room.

Eva Wahl told the PUT director that where the old Oak Hotel stands used to be a Chinese burial ground. The area was excavated for the hotel and tunnels were put in that went from the hotel to the beauty college on Main Street. Resident Jerry Severe tells of going down in the basement of a Chinese restaurant, "The Oregon Café", on Main Street in the 1960's. It sat next to the same beauty college mentioned above. She found old relics, including some Chinese pieces (now on display,) underneath in the tunnels. The tunnels took her under the block and the parking lot where she surfaced in the alley behind The Oak Hotel. The basement of The Oregon Café used to be a card room and enough stories have been confirmed to believe that the Chinese had a swinging panel door for an escape route.

The Chinese would take an unsuspecting cowboy into the basement, steal his money and lean against the panel. It swung around in a circle and would empty the Chinese man into the tunnel system. He could then cross under the street and disappear down several choices of tunnels, leaving a drunk, angry, cowboy behind, still chasing him through the labyrinth below.

There are many stories lost to us and many that we hope will surface in the years ahead. Whether tall or true, all of these stories add to the colorful past of Pendleton's underground.

PART FOUR

Reference Maps, Historic Building Listings and Rare Photos

The maps presented here are based on old city maps and on oral reports. It is interesting to see the differences between the two. We know there is much that has been lost in the way of photos and oral history to complete an accurate picture of how it really was.

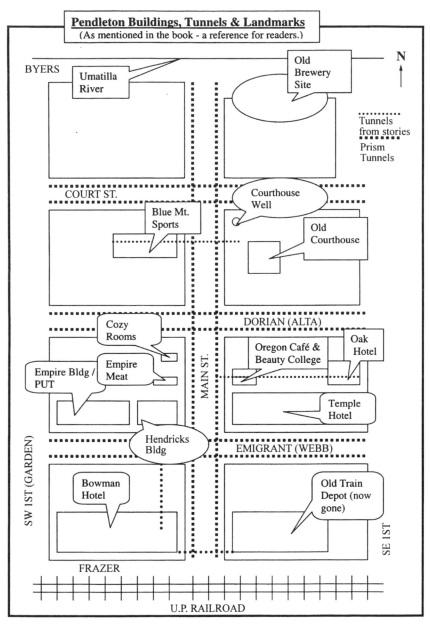

Map of Main Street tunnel system.

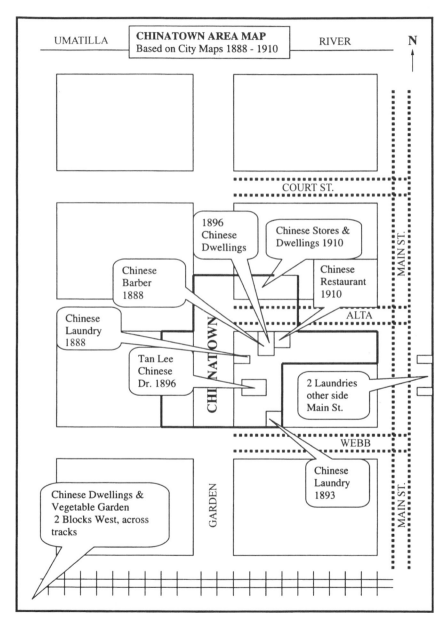

CHINATOWN AREA MAP
Based on City Maps 1888 - 1910

UMATILLA

RIVER

N

COURT ST.

MAIN ST.

1896
Chinese
Dwellings

Chinese Stores &
Dwellings 1910

Chinese
Barber
1888

Chinese
Restaurant
1910

ALTA

Chinese
Laundry
1888

CHINATOWN

Tan Lee
Chinese
Dr. 1896

2 Laundries
other side
Main St.

WEBB

Chinese
Laundry
1893

Chinese Dwellings &
Vegetable Garden
2 Blocks West, across
tracks

GARDEN

MAIN ST.

Map of Chinatown based on city maps.

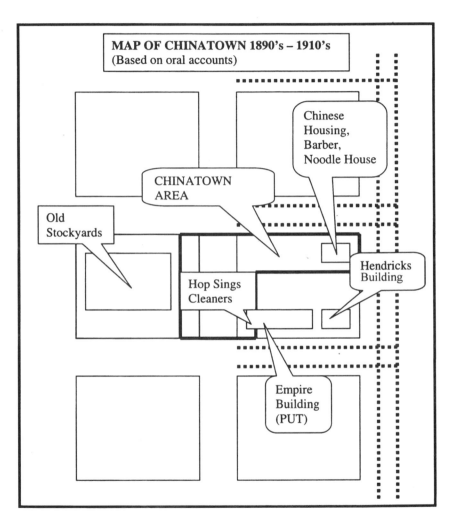

Map of Chinatown based on oral reports.

The photos of the red light district were taken by Bert Arndt in 1982. He took them when he acquired the property. They were part of a collection he used in applying for The National Historic registry.

Olympia Cigar Store sign hangs above Shamrock Card Room sign covering window.

Shamrock Card Room sign close-up.

Olympia Cigar Store and Café, now PUT offices and lobby. To right, arched doorway to Spur Hotel and brothel occupied by Madame Stella Darby from 1953 to 1967.

Old red light district 1982, SW First to Main Street. Note Coca Cola sign.

Rivoli Theater ca. 1930's; mentioned in Introduction by Pam Severe.

Bob's Shoe Shine (Coca Cola sign). Formerly an open alley and entrance to speakeasy.

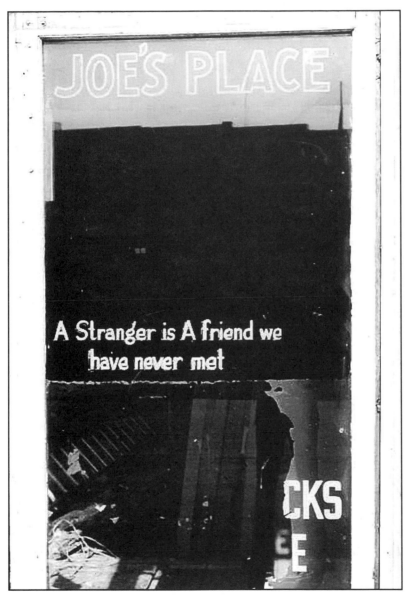

Joe's Place next to Shoe Shine.

51

*Hendricks Building with the Workingmen's Clothing Company, ca. 1900.
Note bowling and pool circle sign. Presently upper floor is
The Working Girls Hotel.*

*Main Street, 3rd block west side of Main Street red light area.
Pendleton Underground Tours travels under this area.*

Historic Buildings Listing and Descriptions

The following buildings were listed on the National Historic Registry in the early 1980's. The buildings listed sit above the underground tour. Some of this information comes from Mr. Arndt's historic registry documentation.

Hendricks Building/New York Store - 1897
C.C. Hendricks, owner of several of Pendleton's bawdy houses, received a patent from the United States of America on the New York Store site in January of 1888. A two-story brick building was constructed in 1897 under Hendricks ownership known as the Hendricks Building. The style is rectangular, two-story commercial with arched windows, flared chimneys and cast iron column front support. Structurally and functionally sound, the building was a clothes store for years called The New York Store and hence its current identity.

The building is situated on the northwest corner of the intersection of Main Street and Emigrant. The New York Store building was originally designed to accommodate two stories on the street level with similarly partitioned basement space. The second story was originally clear span, open space for use by the Macabee Lodge. Later the second floor was remodeled into rooms and the ceiling changed to accommodate skylights. The foundation is irregular basalt rock set in lime mortar.

The original use as can best be constructed was the Bi-jou Saloon in the corner store, a barber shop with baths in the north store, a "duck-pin" bowling alley, pool hall and card room in the basement, and the Knights of the Macabees secret society on the second floor.

The Empire Building & Block - 1907
The Empire Block, constructed in 1907, is an all brick one and two-story commercial building on Emigrant Street. The building's estimated time of construction was 10 years. It was

built as one of several investments of the Schwarz and Greulich Brothers who owned the Empire Meat Company. Empire building retains the only original floor storefronts in the South Main Street Historic District.

The main floor was used for many different businesses over the years—mostly saloons and taverns. During WWII, it was the location for Blackeys Tavern on the corner location. Many buildings in Pendleton had "no black" clauses in their leases until the 1960's so this tavern catered to the black paratroopers stationed at the Pendleton Air Base.

The second floor plans originally called for an opera house with a 9-foot staircase. During construction, the proposed opera house operator came to odds with Schwarz and Greulich and left the project. The design was changed to a boarding house with community baths and toilets. The Spur Hotel was located above the current site of The Pendleton Underground Tours office. It was named the Spur Hotel but it quietly became the Cozy Rooms II until Stella Darby retired in 1967.

The Empire Meat market - 1899

This store on Main Street was constructed as a simple one-story brick store in 1899. A second floor was added in 1912 as a rooming house. The Empire Meat Company was incorporated in 1903 and went through a series of management changes when the four brothers discontinued their partnership. The company was eventually sold outside the family.

Endnotes

1. Nancy E. De Spain, Village Days in Pendleton, "Reminiscences Of Oregon Pioneers", East Oregonian 1937, 3 & 4.

2. Reverend J.M. Cornelison, Reminiscences of a "Young" Pioneer, "Reminiscences Of Oregon Pioneers", East Oregonian 1937, 213.

3. "Souvenir Book, 1899-1900 Pendleton, Umatilla County, Oregon" published 1900, 1.

4. "Souvenir Book, 1899-1900 Pendleton, Umatilla County, Oregon" published 1900, 1.

5. "Souvenir Book, 1899-1900 Pendleton, Umatilla County, Oregon" published 1900, 2.

6. History Of Umatilla County, "Reminiscences of Oregon Pioneers", East Oregonian, 1937, 22.

7. "Souvenir Book, 1899-1900 Pendleton, Umatilla County, Oregon" published 1900, 12.

8. Rufus Crabtree, "The Pendleton Story", Full House Publications 1990, 9 & 10.

9. Gordon Macnab, A Century of News and People in The East Oregonian 1875-1975.

10. Rufus Crabtree, "The Pendleton Story", 53-59.

11. Rufus Crabtree, "The Pendleton Story", 29.

12. Rufus Crabtree, "The Pendleton Story", 29-32.

13. Gordon Macnab, A Century of News and People in The East Oregonian 1875-1975, 69.

14. East Oregonian, Macnab, Gordon. A Century of News and People in The East Oregonian 1875-1975, 96.

15. Blue Mountain Genealogical Society, Blue Mountain Community College, "Golden Yesterdays, A Collection of Reminiscences by Senior Citizens of Umatilla & Morrow Counties". 1982.

16. Blue Mountain Genealogical Society, Blue Mountain Community College, "Golden Yesterdays, A Collection of Reminiscences by Senior Citizens of Umatilla & Morrow Counties". 1982.

17. Dorothy P. Marlow, "Tales of Early Day Orientals In Pendleton", April 1993, PUT archives.

About the Authors

Pam Severe

Pam is a native Pendletonian. After graduating from B.Y.U. in Clothing and Textile, Fashion Merchandising, she never thought she'd be working in the old "red light" district of Pendleton. In 1989, she was a volunteer tour guide and posed in The Shamrock Card Room. In 1991, Pam became the Executive Director of PUT. Her inspiration to publish a book on the Underground's history came from the many tourist requests.

Lon Thornburg

Lon has been a volunteer serving PUT since 1996. He has served on the PUT board, been a tour guide and played the piano in the Shamrock Card Room for PUT "Comes To Life." Lon has helped with entries for the Pendleton Dress-up parade. He has dressed up as the ghost of Mr. Matlock, a turn of the century building owner, for "Hidden Haunts", a benefit tour around Halloween. His background is in the arts and education. He is a teacher in the Pendleton Public Schools. He and his wife's interest in history extend to preserving and operating the 100 year old Meacham Hotel in the Blue Mountains as a group retreat center.